BREAKING THE HABIT OF *OVER* THINKING

The Breakthrough Method for Applying Knowledge Sooner and Taking Aligned Action Faster!

#Quantum Results

CARLA WYNN HALL

BREAKING THE HABIT OF OVERTHINKING

THE BREAKTHROUGH METHOD FOR APPLYING KNOWLEDGE SOONER AND TAKING ALIGNED ACTION FASTER

CARLA WYNN HALL

BREAKING THE HABIT OF *OVERTHINKING*

INTRODUCTION 6
   Becoming a Better Thinker...6
ENGAGING WITH THIS BOOK 9
   Your Free Bonuses..9
GETTING TO KNOW ME..13
   I am a Human Potential Activist..13
   Methodology 15
7 keys to success in action 16
Chapter 1 17
   The Chronic Habit of Overthinking...17
   Neuro Lesson 1 43
Chapter 2 45
   Aligned Action...45
   Neuro Lesson 2 53
Chapter 3 54
   5 Types of Thinkers 54
   Neuro Lesson 3 64
CHAPTER 4 65
   5 Layers of Thinking...65
   Neuro-Lesson 4 75
Chapter 5 77
   Protecting an Idea Like Your Very Life is Completely Depends on It! 77
   Neuro-Lesson 5 86
Chapter 6 87
   Learning to Become a Jedi Master of Idea Generation and Action 87
   Neuro-Lesson 6 98
Chapter 7 99

The Neuroscience of a Thought Process and Endless Feedback Loops 99
Neuro Lesson 7 103
Chapter 8 105
Using Common Sense to Decide when the Thought Can End 105
Neuro-Lesson 8 112
Chapter 9 113
Healing Your Body by Breaking the Habit of Overthinking...........113
Neuro-Lesson 9 118
Final Assessment 119
Conclusion 120
ABOUT THE AUTHOR 122
MEDIA and ORDERS 123

Breaking the Habit of Overthinking

INTRODUCTION

Becoming a Better Thinker

There is one personality characteristic that all leaders share: **They possess the ability to take aligned action quickly.** When they have an idea that appears in their awareness, they quickly analyze the best outcome and take aligned action. Granted, some ideas just are never born, or they are deemed not useable, but great ideas are born, acted upon, and change the world. In Napoleon Hill's "Think and Grow Rich" he speaks of a man who stopped 3-foot short of gold, and because of his decision to stop before he reached his desired goal, he lost everything.

A great thinker will apply knowledge, rather than hoarding it. In the practice of applying knowledge faster, action is taken sooner, and the solution appears clearer.

The Habit of Overthinking is Chronic! The habit of overthinking is an idea stealer and a dream killer. This book was written to bridge the gap between thinking and acting, jumping and falling. It is written for business people, college students, athletes, mothers, fathers, daughters, grandmothers and entrepreneur dreamers. This book is for creative visionaries and political leaders. Breaking the habit of overthinking will open the space for quick resolutions to daunting problems. I will increase your human potential element of conflict resolution, and it will free your body of unwanted stress.

Great ideas are hidden away every day, as they jump from your brain to the brain of someone else who will act sooner. Keep this firmly in your mind; you lose time, money and freedom by being in the habit of overthinking.

We all must think, and we do it a lot! We are crazy thinkers, childish thinkers, drunk thinkers, and creative thinkers. We blend our thoughts with the thoughts of others, and together we create mass chaos then long for clarity. The purpose of this book is to show you how to mass control your thoughts daily and course-correct when needed.

Reading this book will shift the pathways in the brain so be prepared for the transformation of your life, an expansion of your brain's natural power to come to a fast solution, and ideas that flood your mind.

Enjoy.

ENGAGING WITH THIS BOOK

Your Free Bonuses

As a reward for your time reading this book, I have created an online group and course that will support you in detoxing from the habit of overthinking. I will be activating and engaging to areas of your brain to support you in creating new habits, to replace the habit of thinking too much and being stuck the place of a thought with no positive result.

In the pages of this book you will unequivocally learn "The Breakthrough Method for Applying Knowledge Sooner and Taking Aligned Action Faster!" With the nuggets of Neuroscience Principles and the easy roadmap to enlisting the help of your common-sense faculties – you will be a better thinker.

At the end of each chapter, you will be given a three-question exam that helps re-enforce your learning. Answer each question as true as possible so you will retain what you have learned. As you are writing your answers, add some emotion to the answer. For example, if I say, "When can you remember a time when you lost something, because you tried too hard to figure it out?" Answer with the emotions you felt when you lost the thing, person or experience you lost. There is a reason for this, trust me.

FREE BONUSES

- ✓ 3 Part Video Series on Making Fast Decisions

- ✓ Downloadable PDF Workbook to Document Success

- ✓ Free Copy of Think and Grow Rich (Hill) on PDF

- ✓ Free Audio of The Science of Getting Rich (Wattles)

https://www.facebook.com/groups/therichbrain/

NEURO LESSONS

Learn how to retrain and *reprogram* your brain with these lessons designed to create new pathways of thought.

Each lesson is designed to direct you toward a new thought process to apply knowledge faster and succeed sooner.

When you learn the lessons, you can switch easily from a consuming thought, to a productive action.

GETTING TO KNOW ME

I am a Human Potential Activist

Why do I call myself a Human Potential Activist? It's simple. I see potential in everyone from criminals in the prison system, to persons with disabling conditions. I see hope in the hopeless and greatness in the souls of everyone. One area that has been part of my life's mission to master is the area of the brain and how our thoughts, or lack of thoughts, form our reality. Breaking the Habit of Overthinking was born from an idea I had while watching my two sons debate over Shark Tank. During their dramatic conversations, each of them would battle with the other on who was right, and why.

Seriously! As human beings, the habit of overthinking has grown into a plague of sorts. Just as destructive as overthinking is the habit of not thinking at all. We can't go into every detail in this one book, but we will discuss overthinking.

I suffered a concussion in 2017 that took me out of commission for a few months. Even as of the date of this writing 2018, I have short term memory issues and feelings of exhaustion and brain fog. Our brains hold all of the keys to our successes, failures, loves and losses. I hope you enjoy this book as much as I have enjoyed writing it.

This is my 5th published book and the other books I have created can all be found on Amazon.com. My writing style is both practical and metaphysical so enjoy the twists and turns, and find which flavor enjoy the most.

Please take a moment to come to Amazon and review my book. Reviews are the life-blood of authors and imperative to our success in the future.

Carla wynn hall

http://www.TheRichBrain.com (Blog)

Methodology

Neuro Lessons to Stimulate Your Brain

Your brain is wired to do certain things, feel certain emotions, react certain ways. All of the instruction to the rest of your body is created inside of the neuro-walls of the brain. The habit of overthinking, causes the firing of neurons, to get stuck in a single feedback loop, preventing you from going to another thought properly, and from making critical decisions faster.

Overthinking is not a bad thing, it's a normal thing. Our methodology will help you to get through thought processes faster, but applying knowledge sooner thus freeing your brain space for another thought.

The Breakthrough Method for Applying Knowledge Sooner and Taking Aligned Action Faster!

This method teaches you how to intentionally get out of any thought that is living too long in your brain and to take aligned action faster. The sooner you move from thought and idea, to action and application, the sooner you will create and attract the situations and money you want and desire to possess.

7 KEYS TO SUCCESS IN ACTION

1. Identify the Thought
2. Research the Options
3. Decide to Act
4. Clarify Your Results
5. Remove Negative Results
6. Reboot the Idea
7. Complete the Feedback Loop

CHAPTER 1

The Chronic Habit of Overthinking

'One of the most common causes of failure is the habit of quitting when one is overtaken by temporary defeat. Every person is guilty of this mistake at one time or another."

Napoleon Hill (Think and Grow Rich)

IDENIFYING A THOUGHT – The first step to finding Success Sooner! To break the habit of overthinking through utilizing the formula I have created for you, it's academically sound, for you to begin practicing the formula with a goal to break the habit of overthinking, the mental addictions that go with overthinking. Identifying thought is the first step. Knowing what you are thinking about allows you to draw from the storage of knowledge and applying it quicker.

Welcome to "Breaking the Habit of Overthinking". This book will form the basis of a foundation you create for yourself, that allows you to think more powerfully, with less time stuck in the thought, and more time taking massive, aligned action – SOONER. The lessons are clearly designed to show you how to use applied knowledge to attract what you want in life.

I am going to show you how the habit of overthinking, could be the single most important clue you have into why you feel unsuccessful. Breaking this habit connects your true desires, with the best actions.

There is a chronic epidemic of overthinking that needs to be fully addressed. Napoleon Hill said it right when he quoted that "One of the most common causes of failure is quitting when one is overtaken by temporary defeat. – Hill (Think and Grow Rich). In the exact moment that your thoughts go toward quitting, you have lost. *Thinking can never stop but mastering the quality of your thoughts can be a life-long achievement.*

A Visualization

Imagine you are walking on a pond that is frozen, and the ice begins to crack open. You can hear the ice crackling around you and fear that you will fall if the ice continues to crack. You think to yourself, "What is the temperature today?", and "What is the likelihood that the ice will crack?". Then you think, "If I fall into the hole, how long would it take before I froze to death". In the 2 minutes it took you to think about the options and possibilities, the ice doesn't crack. But, you have felt it crack in your mind, and you have agreed that you probably were over-thinking.

Choose which things you give lengthy thought to, and which things you will take quick, aligned action toward. In the 2 minutes you were debating over the ice, you could have fallen into the cold water and froze to death. Yes! This is serious.

Your brain has been programmed to think the way you do, and it's not all your fault that you are in the habit of overthinking. Your brain is so trainable; it's like a pink sponge, hungry for your input. Each time you intentionally work on what your brain does for you, you create a new path for your brain to follow.

At the end of each chapter I have given you a "Neuro-Lessons" to complete with the intention that you expand your brain's capacity to take in knowledge, and quickly use it to attract what you want in life. These lessons form the foundation of the "Breakthrough Method" I am providing to you here. Each lesson is designed to stretch your brain, and learn the real secret to success, shared by the world's foremost experts in the field.

A Million Thoughts

We have millions of thoughts each day, and our brain processes them and stores them for retrieval sometime in the future. Overthinking is simply going past the point of no return with a thought. At the apex of a thought there is only 1 right choice.

Thinking is normal and without thought, you would not be able to make decisions and you would probably be a jellyfish. Your thoughts come to you based on many factors, some even were implanted in you before your birth. One of the greatest thoughts you can have is that of a simple idea. Ideas give us an expanded version of what is, and what could be. Ideas are knocks on your door, beaconing you to take aligned action.

Breaking any habit requires a new habit to be added. With new habits come new thought pathways.

As you are breaking the habit of overthinking, be vigilant about the new thought you put into your brain. Remember, this book is not meant to convince you to not think, nor is it meant to convince you that thinking is bad. It is the sincere hope that this book will convince you how to **quickly think** with authority, take swift and aligned action, then jump with the idea, becoming a master and the short, intentional thought. Breaking the generational chronic habit of overthinking, will require you to ask yourself what thoughts are keeping you stuck, keeping you safe, and keeping you in a tailspin.

THE PARALYZING PAUSE

In my 10 years of being on online entrepreneur, human potential activist and award-winning author, I have witnessed too many times, people who never take a toe forward toward their dreams, for being stuck in a relentless "Pause". It is in this paralyzing pause, that opportunities are missed and possible danger creeps in around you. In the business world, being stuck in the paralysis of analysis, can mean your business may fail because of your inability to make fast decisions. When I say the chronic habit of overthinking, through the concept of this book, I am saying that you put too much unnecessary thought into almost all of your everyday interactions, and by doing so, you are creating an ecosystem of thoughts with no solution.

Basing my Authority on Experience

In my line of work with women writers, and as a Human Potential Activist and Idea Activator, I am always confronted with situations where people simply miss the best parts of their life because they cannot get out of their heads. By out of their heads, I mean spinning in an endless, non-productive feedback loop, unable to take one step toward the realization and attraction found inside their minds.

I have to be honest, it was not easy to decide to write this book. My hands were shaking, as a matter of fact. Writing about deeper topics that impact an entire society, always invokes fear, but fear is now my nitro. How can we stop thinking too much? Will that make us Jellyfish? Will people embrace or repel the notion of breaking the habit of overthinking?

Yes, all these doubts entered into my mind, as I too was engaging in the same habit we are going to break.

Like you, I worry about what people think of me, whether I will be up to the level of other great authors, and whether or not I can sell a single book. I published my first book "The Rock Bottom Chronicles" solo, in 2014, through an outfit for self-publishing. As an Indie (Independent Author), I had no idea how I would pull it off. As I began to think about writing a book, I didn't act fast. In fact, I cried because I could not figure out how I could make it happen. I lamented every day about wanting to write a book but would never start.

Eventually, I was *drawn into action* by the thoughts swirling in my mind. The dream started to move me and pull my thoughts upward toward concentrated and aligned action. As I was pecking out my book, the desire to tell my story and heal through writing, started to be far more important than my fear of letting it out. In my decision to take aligned action, meaning *my actions fully aligned with my inner-desire*, I became a published author. I said, "My book will be a #1 New York Times Bestselling Book".

I worked, typed, cried, typed some more and cried some more. No, my book did not become a bestseller of any sort but "The Rock Bottom Chronicles" gave me a hunger to continue writing books. This book, in your hand, is the 5th published book I will have had my hands on and I don't ever plan on stopping.

> *"There is never a shortage of the need for good books to be published and accessible to generations of readers" – Carla*

The greatest books in the world, were written by people who had a big idea and took action quickly. Jack Canfield, author of Chicken Soup for the Soul, says to take action on any hunch, even if it seems impossible.

Can you repeat after me? I will make this happen. I want to say yes to this opportunity. I believe that I am feeling the right YES to get me to a new level. Saying yes is the first step, but you will be tempted to quit, and you will want to turn around and run.

2-Feet from Gold – The Story of Overthinking and Losing Money

Maybe you have read the book "Think and Grow Rich" and read the story of the man who stopped 3-feet from Gold and in his stopping, he lost millions of dollars in money, present and future. You are 2-feet from gold and you are about to lose everything you have worked for. The dream you have chased, has hidden away in the high-grass. It peeps out at you every now and then, as you are stuck in over-planning, not acting, not moving and not deciding. You are about to stop short of your blessing.

As you think about the success that awaits you, and you decide to chance, you will no longer stop short of gold, but you will keep digging. Remember, overthinking is a habit, and it can be changed. In the story of the gold rush where a man stopped just 3-Feet from gold, we have a condition where he thought he know the right location to dig and left the work unfinished. Did he engage in the habit of overthinking, or did he fail to continue based on his desire to quit?

What are Habits?

Overthinking is a habit that millions of people share. A habit, as you may or may not know, is an unconscious behavior that people engage in and the only way to change a habit is with another habit. Here is where this book title is going to trick your brain and trick the universe. To break the habit of overthinking, you must learn to take aligned action sooner. Aligned action is action taken as the result of a hunch, or idea. An idea is living inside of you like a baby being incubated in the mother's womb. When you have an idea and you do not act on it, you may be voluntarily giving that idea to another person. And, in not taking action toward your hunch, and giving your idea away, you could be giving up amenities like money and fame. So, let's work through this concept.

I intentionally added the passage from Think and Grow Rich called "Stopping 3-Feet from Gold" to show you what you can lose by staying in a non-productive thought pattern; your habit of overthinking is part of a pattern.

The chronic habit of overthinking prevents you from moving forward. To give you some examples of what over thinking can do, look at these 4 potential situations of over-thinking.

1. When you have a business proposal that involves a substantial cost, and you can't get past the cost, into the space of benefit. You lament over the choice for weeks, until the opportunity goes away. In the book Big Magic written by Liz Gilbert, she talks candidly about an idea that came to her, she ignored it, and someone else picked it up energetically. She allowed the idea t to leave her. If you are in the no habit and want to be in the yes habit, try the action step below.

    a. The Remedy is to take aligned action and to discover the ROI well before you see it in your reality. If an opportunity comes to you, take it. Say YES with courage and bravery.

2. You go onto Shark Tank with your company. Your company has barely started up and you are eager to get the shark's money. You prepare the speech, practice the pitch, perfect your presentation and rebuttals. You are all ready, or so you think. As you get in front of the sharks your skin begins to

curl. You are afraid they will offer to take too much equity. You don't want to give up any more equity than you think is appropriate. To your surprise, an offer is made and it's slightly more than you want to let go of. But, inside you are pretty sure you cannot fulfil your dream without the investment. Your habit of chronic overthinking, may have cost you your investment.

- a. Your pause cost you an investment from the sharks because you took too long thinking about it and didn't take aligned action toward the yes. I took a year and watched every episode of Shark Tank in existence, so I could be well-versed on this topic and book.

3. You think 5-seconds too long when deciding to turn your car onto a major road. This one is a bit emotional. In your insistence on thinking about the variables of shifting sand, you turn and don't see the 18-wheeler coming right at you. No, the truck doesn't hit you because you sped up when you saw it coming. No, you didn't get crushed to oblivion, but you almost did. There is a time and place for over-thinking.

- a. Each time you approached this road after that day, you payed extra attention to how you felt about the decision to pull out, rather than trying to logically figure out whether traffic will be coming.

Overthinking is the habit of going from thought to thought with no possible solution in sight. Your job today is to say yes to something spontaneously without thinking about the results.

What is Applied Knowledge?

Part of the breakthrough system I am teaching you in this book, is to use Knowledge as an Application and do it swiftly. This section focuses on taking thoughts, adding action and succeeding sooner.

Knowledge Hoarding

With Google and the hundreds of ways you can learn new things, it's super easy to hoard knowledge and never use it. You may find that you take classes that cost thousands of dollars, never to use one of them. You may click and sign up for every freebie you can get your hands on, and never read one of them. This is knowledge hoarding. Applied knowledge is taking what you learn and acting on it fast.

There are times when fast action is a safety precaution as in the examples in the previous section, but using applied knowledge carries the same principles. First, none of the knowledge you hold, will ever benefit you if you don't use it for betterment of self-and community. When you knowledge hoard, and you don't access the right action, then take it, you will be stuck in overthinking mode.

Types of Overthinking

Overthinking and Relationships

Have you ever heard someone say to you, "I'm just trying to figure it out"? You can bet that the person who is figuring it out, may never figure it out. Overthinking in relationships can be harmful to the union, and even cause it to end. There is only so much a single thought can do, thus each thought must have a visible solution that can be reached quickly. In relationships, a two-way dialogue is needed to sustain the relationship. When one party is spontaneous and has the urge to do things quickly, while the other wants to figure out all of the details, the relationship may get watered down. This causes the partners to lose their communication feedback loop.

In the breakdown of communication, the relationship begins to decay. There are a few ways to lessen the blow dealt by chronic thought addiction, and they require eye-to-eye contact and a mutual understanding of the desired result.

I feel prepared to write this book, because I have experienced chronic overthinkers my whole life. 2 of them are my sons. My two sons, at the time of this writing, are ages 20 and 16. Their whole life, they have been homeschooled. They are each other's best friends. But they think about everything to the nano-fact. They talk all day long about figuring out different things such as the next Nintendo game to release, or how to make better dumplings.

Now, I never try to cramp their obsessive thought habits because they are still trying to figure out their entire life starting with the present-day moment, what the future holds. I do, however, stop them when it starts to go too far. I ask them to create something such as a drawing, or simply go outside and get some air. I watch as their curiosity turns to something similar to an argument, then becomes a bit charged. I laugh because they have the brains of geniuses, and their conversations are so deep.

Overthinking and Missed Business Opportunity

Without a doubt, in business, taking aligned action quickly may be the straw that breaks the camel's back in your business success. Learning to cap the thought with inspired action can take your business from a mere plan, to a successful venture. Taking the knowledge, you acquire through life, and alchemizing it into application, you are clearing space for more creative awareness in your business. Overthinking opportunities, can cause you to lose the game, before the dice is rolled.

CASE STUDY: THE $50 DEAL

As an example, I will tell you about a service that I have provided for several years. Many entrepreneurs want to be published authors, they know their public is looking for their book, yet they refuse to jump. My company has created book writing programs priced at only $50 to join; less than a latte a day, right? The people who show up to this opportunity, will think about the timeline, think about their commitments, think about the reasonability of their commitment. They never invest. They love and feel the idea, are excited about the opportunity, then they start to think. In an endless feedback loop of thinking of the reasons not to say yes, they lose the opportunity and the idea is put away.

It's in their inability to take aligned action sooner, that they lose the opportunity to become a published author. They don't see their ROI attaching to a small investment. They don't see all of the amazing things they can do with their book after it publishes. They don't see the benefit of group thinking and mentorship. All they see are the millions of ways they can talk themselves out of taking part in the program.

Breaking the Habit of Overthinking through NLP

If you are one of the millions of online superheroes creating solutions for businesses, or personally coaching individuals then you must close sales in order to keep your company or business alive, and you must close these sales in an amount sufficient to sustain your needs and desires. To do this, it's your duty to speak to people and decide what words to use, that convince the prospect quickly to buy your products. There are many ways to learn how to weave your words so that your offers are delicious and irresistible.

We have briefly spoken of breaking the habit of overthinking for yourself, but I want to introduce the concept of NLP to you, so you can break this habit on your client's behalf and give them reasons to joyfully say YES to making a decision to buy from you. This is going to go into mind work so switch off your thought box for a moment and try to feel your way through the next few paragraphs. I know you can do this. I believe in you.

In 2016 my youngest sister Apryl was killed in a car accident. She was addicted to pain medications since the age of 8 when she developed painful childhood arthritis. Because of her addiction, her life took her down many dark paths into deeper and harder addictions.

Feeling as if she was not accepted, she would often wail to die. She didn't want to be in her body. It hurt too much, and she could not break the addiction.

Not only did she get into heavy drugs, but she got into very unsafe behavior. I love and miss her every day. She and I were not close, because I could not be around the behavior she exhibited when she was truly high; all I could do is pray. Then the day came when she gave up her body and went home to be with our grandparents. She had finally changed her life. At her memorial service a group of women came in like a scene in a movie. It was her rehab home buddies and they had come to celebrate their friend.

In a conversation after the birthday service memorial – my sister died 8 days before her birthday – they told me she saved their life.

Listening to the Inner Voice

The inner voice is what guides you to make decisions sooner and take aligned action faster. It's the idea trying to nudge you. It's the instruction to say YES when you really want to "Think about it". I listened to my inner voice that rang through a brain full of self-imposed expectations I had placed upon myself. The inner voice also tries to give you a hint that it's time to use your knowledge.

I was at dinner with my family, and I had tried to set a cardinal rule to not answer Facebook messages while at dinner. I looked at the message, thought about it for a few seconds, even turned off my phone, for about 2-minutes, then something gave me a twinge. I turned my phone back on, replied to the message, setup a phone call, made the phone call and closed the deal.

In the beginning of this chapter, I told you the story of my sister's passing to say this: The connecting thread was that my client was working with recovering addicts in an intense program to heal those who had been long term addicted to drugs, alcohol, sex, food – you name it. Our conversation also leads to a plan that would help fulfil my dream of taking a writing program into jails, prisons, rehab centers, halfway houses and mental health facilities.

"Remember, all prospects were first humans. They have something you can connect with to convince them to not overthink. With my client, it was my ability to be raw and talk about my story". CWH

Procrastination and chronic overthinking go hand in hand.

Procrastination is putting off until tomorrow, what should be done today. Usually when someone is in the heat of procrastination, they also are overthinking some part of the situation. Procrastination is taking a deliberate pause, so you can fact-find a bit more, pretend to have a conflict, or intentionally put off an answer. Sometimes the

"Procrastination Pause" is merited, the majority of the time, procrastination waters down potential results.

The only thought stopping you from saying yes to something you procrastinate about – is the fear of the unknown. Each fear attaches to a belief, and you know the story from there. **When you really want to achieve a goal, yet you have not logged any action steps, you will never achieve your goal.** When you fail to say yes, without looking at the reality of a no, you toss out potential. When you say no, you are cutting off the feedback loop of receiving the benefits of saying yes.

Procrastination is when you wait so long to say yes that the idea is ripped from you and given to someone else. Decisions require thought, and we are not saying to go through life and not think at all. We are saying that the sooner you make an inspired, decisive and empowered action (IDEA) the sooner your brain can go on to form a new pathway from the thought (or idea in your head) to the end result of which you can craft and visualize during a span of a few minutes. If you can visualize the end result of your action, in a span of only a few minutes as opposed to a few days, weeks or even months, you are able to see results faster.

Remember, every choice you make leads to another choice. In the year 2017 my family had a unique opportunity to say yes, to taking aligned action sooner, when we were going to Chattanooga, Tennessee to eat lunch. Let me tell you this cute story that will warm your heart and help you believe in the power of aligned action.

Meeting Santa Claus

My husband is a disabled USAF Veteran and is the love of my life. After 3 failed marriages on his side, and 2 failed marriages on mine, we came together in odd circumstances. He and I met each other on Plenty of Fish or (POF), which is a dating site on the Internet. I had just blazed through two relationships with men, and by all opinions, should have just gave it up. In my darkest night of the soul, with one eye open and one eye closed, I said YES to a single profile, after 2-hours of saying no, and a lot of bad words to creeps on there who were just icky.

I had made a list of non-negotiables which included no smoking or tobacco, 6' 4", Blue Eyes and (No Harley Motorcycles) or a photo holding a fish. Well, he was and is 6' 4" and he does have blue eyes, but he dipped tobacco and had a Harley motorcycle AND his profile picture was of him holding a damned fish.

So, that night, with my contacts as dry as a desert, I met someone else on POF – my Future Husband. Everything in me wanted to say no, but something deeper within me said "He is the One". I wrestled with saying yes but did agree to meet him. The reason I chose to say yes was that he wrote complete sentences and with poise. We were married on Valentine's Day, 2014 and to the date of this writing, we have been married for 4-years. So, "How does Santa Claus" fit into this, you may ask. The story of how my husband became "Santa Bear" is all about taking fast and aligned action when the opportunity presents itself to you.

In August of 2017, my husband was offered what he saw as his dream job, doing CAD (Computer Aided Drawing) for a local land surveying company. He was making $400 a week straight cash, and I thought it was incredible. Disabled Veterans don't have a good track record of finding good employment.

We were all in Chattanooga, Tennessee, my husband, my sons and me. That day, we were about to go eat at a local Chinese Restaurant when we got a call from Alabama, where my husband's family lives, that my husband's great-grandmother was about to die. No, she didn't die, she is still aggressively kicking, but here's why this is important. We were standing 2-feet from gold that day because we were delayed in our plans. That 20-minute delay was for a reason.

As we began to walk into the restaurant, someone who looked just like the Big Guy, was coming out of the restaurant. He was grinning from ear-to-ear as I snickered to my sons, "He got stopped by Santa". My sons and I continued inside as my husband and the Santa man shook hands and started to talk. I started to really wonder what the conversation was all about and knew my husband could talk someone's ears right off of their head.

As my husband walked into the room, he had this jolly look on his face. He said, "Guess who I just met?". I replied, "Santa". He replied by handing me a business card that read "Santa Rick. Professional Santa for Hire". It was true. He had met Santa Claus. Now, here is where we are going to talk about why you must break the habit of overthinking and jump when the opportunity comes to you.

Santa Rick told my husband to get with him at the first of October because there was going to be a meeting of the "Tri-State Santa" group and he wanted my husband to attend the meeting. My husband put the card in his wallet and left it there. He took aligned action when he started seriously considering being a professional Santa and the joys it would bring. He took further action by considering this opportunity as something real and valuable. But, the "Santa Card" remained in his pocket. That is, until the day he lost his job. On September 30th, my husband was let go of his job. He was almost devastated. That was, until he pulled out the "Santa Card", and like magic, our life changed.

We did the 2017 season as a very green "Mr. and Mrs. Claus". We helped about 40 children feel the magic of Christmas because we said

YES and followed the Universal trail of gifts, tangible and intangible. We got so much free food, it's not even funny.

One of the gigs we did as Mr. and Mrs. Claus was at Pizza Hut in our local community. The manager MaryAnn and her mama Grannie – took us in when we first moved to the community. Santa had a great day and talked to many children. A few months later, Santa was hired to work at Pizza Hut after months of job searching.

When you take aligned action on an idea, you are telling the Universe that you want more and can be more, with more.

10 Tricks to Overcome Overthinking and Prevent Mind Clogs and Migraines from Thinking Too Much!

1. Become aware of your overthinking.

Before you can begin to address or cope with your habit of overthinking, you need to learn to be aware of it when it's happening. Any time you find yourself doubting or feeling stressed or anxious, step back and look at the situation and how you're responding. In that moment of awareness is the seed of the change you want to make.

Sitting with your eyes closed, with your hand on your head, is a red flag letting you know that you are overthinking.

2. Don't think of what can go wrong, but what can go right.

In many cases, overthinking is caused by a single emotion: fear. When you focus on all the negative things that might happen, it's easy to become paralyzed. Next time you sense that you starting to spiral in that direction, stop. Visualize all the things that can go right and keep those thoughts present and up front. Saying YES fast, and on purpose, starts to dismantle the fear of the decision.

3. Distract yourself into happiness.

Sometimes it's helpful to have a way to distract yourself with happy, positive, healthy alternatives. Things like mediation, dancing, exercise, learning an instrument, knitting, drawing, and painting can distance you from the issues enough to shut down the over analysis.

4. Put things into perspective.

It's always easy to make things bigger and more negative than they need to be. The next time you catch yourself making a mountain out of a molehill, ask yourself how much it will matter in five years. Or, for that matter, next month. Just this simple question, changing up the time frame, can help shut down overthinking.

5. Stop waiting for perfection.

This is a big one. For all of us who are waiting for perfection, we can stop waiting right now. Being ambitious is great but aiming for perfection is unrealistic, impractical, and debilitating. The moment you start thinking "This needs to be perfect" is the moment you need to remind yourself, "Waiting for perfect is never as smart as making progress."

6. Change your view of fear.

Whether you're afraid because you've failed in the past, or you're fearful of trying or overgeneralizing some other failure, remember that just because things did not work out before does not mean that has to be the outcome every time. Remember, every opportunity is a new beginning, a place to start again.

7. Put a timer to work.

Give yourself a boundary. Set a timer for five minutes and give yourself that time to think, worry, and analyze. Once the timer goes off, spend 10 minutes with a pen and paper, writing down all the things that are worrying you, stressing you, or giving you anxiety. Let it rip. When the 10 minutes is up, throw the paper out and move on--preferably to something fun.

8. Realize you can't predict the future.

No one can predict the future; all we have is now. If you spend the present moment worrying about the future, you are robbing yourself of your time now. Spending time on the future is simply not productive. Spend that time instead on things that give you joy.

9. Accept your best.

The fear that grounds overthinking is often based in feeling that you aren't good enough--not smart enough or hardworking enough or dedicated enough. Once you've given an effort your best, accept it as such and know that, while success may depend in part on some things you can't control, you've done what you could do.

10. Be grateful.

You can't have a regretful thought and a grateful thought at the same time, so why not spend the time positively? Every morning and every evening, make a list of what you are grateful for. Get a gratitude buddy and exchange lists so you have a witness to the good things that are around you.

Overthinking is something that can happen to anyone. But if you have a great system for dealing with it you can at least ward off some of the negative, anxious, stressful thinking and turn it into something useful, productive, and effective.

In Chapter One I have given you some very valuable life-skills that support your decision to Break the Habit of Overthinking. In Chapter Two we are going to talk about the "Art of Jumping and Taking Aligned Action Sooner" In this chapter, we will briefly discuss the neuroscience of a thought not acted upon and the common sense of taking action – simply to end the thought process for your own brain's health.

Thank you for reading Chapter 1 – You Rock!

Neuro Lesson 1

 **NEURO LESSONS**

Please use your journal to do this lesson. I want to ask you to do this lesson with an open mind, and a willing heart. Breaking the habit of overthinking is going to engage your brain to form start and stop points for every valuable and viable thought. *HINT* Writing immediately breaks the thought process in the head and brings it to life.

Answer the Following Questions:

1. What is an opportunity that has been presented to you through an idea, that you said no to, and ended up regretting?

2. When have you said yes too quickly, and ended up regretting that decision?

Each of these questions can also be answered in the Neuro Lab group on Facebook. There are 1000's of members who are all practicing Breaking the Habit of Overthinking.

CHAPTER 2

Aligned Action

"When you have inspired thought, you have to trust it and you have to act on it." Jack Canfield

As I taught you in Chapter 1, taking Aligned Action means feeling a hunch, or idea, then taking one step toward this idea becoming real. I also told you that failing to do so, could mean giving away money, freedom, fame and opportunity. Aligned action is like knocking on the Universe's door and asking to come into a store with unlimited shelf space, where you have the "Gold Card" to grab what you like on your journey. This means jumping, even afraid.

Just as Mr. Jack Canfield, creator of Chicken Soup for the Soul says, "You must take action when you have an inspired thought". The Habit of Overthinking often prevents inspired thoughts from converting into aligned action. In my work, I am a sales woman, and because I must convert a conversation into a paid contract, I will ask for the sale sooner. This is not a trait that came natural to me, but one I learned how to master. The reactions I got from prospects I was attempting to sell as service to – were often tainted with ridiculous reasons why they had to say no. I heard everything from "I have to ask my husband", to "I don't know if I have the time".

Breaking a habit must start with creating a new habit. Dismantling a pattern filled with backwards habits is even harder. Social media has provided a unique opportunity for miscommunication, and serious mind control. What is said on social interfaces such as Facebook, is often accepted as the "Golden Rule". I have witnessed thousands of new ideas and instructions on what constitutes normal. From how to create and build a bigger email list, to how many times to post or not to post. When you are attempting to be a YES person, you must find some things and say yes to them, even if you try to guilt yourself into saying no.

If overthinking is a habit that is chronic, then the new habit to create is thinking and acting smarter, faster. Rather than deliberating for days on the answer to a question, try to deliberate for 12 hours, then make a decision. Instilling new habits requires you to unearth a new habit then repeat it until it becomes default, replacing the old habit.

Failure to Launch

Someone I met on social media several years ago, had gotten a money inheritance from her adopted father, and her intention was to use that money to improve her life, take some coaching, write a book and create a business. Every day she would message me with a different problem going on with her coaching, her book, or her life. She remained skeptical through every contact.

I watched as she spent money upwards of $100,000 on more training that she never acted on – she was in **perpetual failure to launch**. She wrote her book, had copies made, did multiple book signings and had celebrity access. She even had access to Jack Canfield on several occasions – yet she never launched. Her insistence on overthinking, cost her a career in mindset and business strategy consulting because she could not quit trying to figure it out.

Overthinking is a chronic disease of the mind. It's an endless runway of options upon options, with no obvious solution. In her case, it ended her up broke and searching for plain work at the lowest level of her knowledge and skills.

Learning How to Create the Yes Habit

The case study above was one that is not uncommon in the realm of online businesses. In fact, it seems to be very common among the crowd of business people I hang around with. Since there are so many options for training, planning and launching, a savvy idea generator "YOU", may be faced with some scary choices to make. In the case above, you may ask, "What would have happened if she would have launched sooner, and taken her idea to the masses, even with the deep fear of failure?

Consumer Experiences

Being in the habit of over analyzing everything, puts a consumer in a disadvantage. Oftentimes, people will start out saying no, simply to buy the time for even more reasons to say know. When you are being asked to buy something, you have two choices: Find the yes faster, or be tangled in the possibilities of everything that could go wrong.

Being approached to buy something often puts you in the mental capacity of saying no quick, then putting the seller in a position to negotiate. In your insistence to say NO to the seller, you are in fact saying no to your growth. If you are a consumer of products online, then you have met a freelance worker or someone who is trying to sell you something. You may have really wanted to jump but retreated instead. A good way to instill a new habit is to just go out thee and say yes to something that is attractive.

Udemy Online Learning Academy

Because learning is truly a lifetime process, I go out and plow the Internet for things I want to learn. Recently, the company Udemy, which offers 100's of learning courses, had a special. All their courses were $11.99 and included topics such as Neuroscience and Cognitive

Behavior Therapy Certification. These are all topics, as you can see, which I am completely passionate about. I saw the special come in through my email inbox, and the hunch started. It felt like a warm rush of oxygen through my body. Then, the habit of overthinking started to creep in. "Do I need these? Should I spend the money? Will I finish?". Since I have trained myself on breaking this habit, I quickly clicked the link and started to pick out my classes.

The more I clicked, the more the feeling of warmth penetrated my core. I wanted to expand my knowledge. Expanding my knowledge, would help me be a better person. Having more knowledge on important topics in human development, would help me to write this book. Writing this book, would give me another book toward my life's dream of retiring from book royalty, as a rich, self-published author.

I lovingly nurtured the hunch, acted and signed up for 4 classes. And, I only paid $11.99 for each of them. The next day, the same classes were $199.00. Do you see the importance of me taking quick aligned action, listening to the intuition of my body, and making the jump? This is how you begin to replace the habit of chronic overthinking, with a new habit of trusting yeses that come from your core.

The Neuroscience of a Renegade and Unresolved Thought

Recently, I have been engulfed in learning about the human brain and its connection with our reality. As I explained above, I registered for several classes to help me understand how the human brain works in different situations.

After suffering a traumatic brain injury in February of 2017, I realized just how sensitive yet strong the brain truly is. Without going into detail about this event, I want to talk to you about "The Science of Thinking". Don't worry, you can read all about my head injury in "How to Bend the YOUniverse: Feeling Totality Through the Experience" (Available on my Website).

What is "The Science of Thinking"? The biology of a thought and the anatomy of a thought pattern, are the actual movement of energy through the brain, into the heart and through the system of core beliefs you hold inside of you. Your understanding of this topic, will certainly help you want to break the habit of overthinking, so you can break the thought pattern of saying no. Breaking the thought pattern of saying no, supports you in saying yes to your creativity and ability to enjoy your choices more.

In a University of Berkley research project, they were able to discover the activity inside of the brain, during surgery on someone with epilepsy and found that the frontal vortex of the brain, remained active in trying to reach a solution, all the way through the surgery. Using advanced technology, the findings were similar to what I am saying, that a thought that cannot be resolved, can cause endless Stuckness.

"Some of the responding areas lit up remarkably early, often during the stimulus, suggesting that even before we have a complete response handy, our brain is already getting those parts of the cortex ready for action."

https://www.sciencealert.com/neuroscience-tracking-thoughts-through-brain-prefrontal-cortex-role

Since your brain is constantly preparing for action, it's your responsibility to take care of what your brain needs. Act with your consciousness. Do it faster. This helps your brain flow better for you and continue to open up new pathways to endless opportunities.

Recognizing when you are in the grips of Overthinking

I can tell easily when the overthinking monster is around because I will find myself in an endless feedback look of, "What if". I will be trying to analyze ever situation and figure out every solution. Finding myself with my hand on my brow, is the red-light for me that I must stand up and take action. Overthinking wastes our precious time. Now, I am not saying to not think at all, for some degree of thinking must always be present, les we run out into oncoming traffic with slobber flowing down our face. Thinking and overthinking are two very different things.

Would you agree that today, you have access to answers to any question you may have on any subject that interests you? With this landscape in front of us, we tend to have a wandering mind, and are very slow to reach deep decisions that are very impactful in our experience.

Rather than empowering us to make better choices, our virtually unlimited access to information often leads to greater fear of making the wrong decision, which in turn leads to us spinning our wheels in a seemingly inescapable purgatory of analysis paralysis, all the while getting nowhere on our important projects. You literally could be up all night long researching the neuroscience of inner engineering.

Chapter 2 was focused on aligned action and the victory of saying YES to more opportunities in life. Saying yes means ending a thought pattern, by simply giving into the possibility of success, by saying YES. The most powerful action step you can take, is to say yes to something, more often than you say no to something.

Thank you for reading Chapter 2 – You are so awesome!

Neuro Lesson 2

To protect your brain from being trapped, and to influence your tribe to trust you – you must break the Habit of Overthinking. Here are three action steps you can use when thinking about something.

1. Say to yourself, "What is the best result I can think of, from the thought I am having today? Then write this down in a whole and complete sentence.

2. Read out loud, what you just wrote on your paper. How do you feel about the best result you can think of for the thought you are having?

3. Take a breath and decide what to do. When you have decided what to do, write it down and end it with "And So It Is", then trust your intuition that has delivered you the answer.

CHAPTER 3

5 Types of Thinkers

Calculating Your Maximum Thinking Personality Blend based on the type of thinker you have been and type of thinker you want to be.

What type of thinker are you? Perhaps you are a research hound and like to know every single aspect of a transaction before saying yes. You may be a non-thinker and prefer to engage in mind-numbing activity most of your days. Or, if you are like me, you think long enough for the idea to immerge and then you take swift action. No matter which type of thinker you are, you probably could use some help breaking the habit of overthinking. Remember, we are not trying to get you to stop thinking, but to engage daily, in powerful thinking. We are not trying to make you change the type of thinker you are, but the type of thinker you are becoming.

The Genius Thinker

Innovation begins with a need. Whether it's a new way to communicate across the world, or a solution to relieve fidgeting, all innovation starts with a need. The "Genius Thinker" runs 24-7, on pure, inventive adrenaline. This type of thinker can see an improvement in almost anything. They have constant flows of ideas coming to them every day.

My two sons are "Genius Thinkers" I suspect they inherited this from me, or perhaps their father, but they are constantly churning out new ways to do things. Nickolas loves Nintendo games and he is always looking for the latest "reveal" or game hack, looking at ways to improve the animation or the characters in the game. Him and his brother Joshua invent recipes for different food items and their talks when we are all in a vehicle together, are 99% about the many ways to do or improve things within their computer games.

Genius thinkers are sometimes hard to get along with because they are inside of their innovation all day and night. They can take anything that exists and find a way to expand and improve products, processes and packaging. They are very detailed. Contrary to what you may thing, "Genius Thinkers" are very right-brained (Creative Thinking) and not so much left-brained (Organizational Thinking).

The Sluggish Thinker

Brain injury causes life-long brain fog: People who suffer from traumatic brain injury are sluggish thinkers. And, so are those who consume too much alcohol or take drugs. This type of thinker will stay inside of a loose thought and spin themselves into confusion. A "Sluggish Thinker" has characteristics of being perpetually confused and will need reassurance and reminders about everything. They are often disconnected with many conversations.

Traumatic brain injury is a condition where the brain is loosened from the skull, resulting in a mis-firing of the neurons inside of the brain. When this disruption occurs, many symptoms follow. As the brain begins to remember its core instructions, clarity and focus. Memories stored inside of the brain, may be lost or re-organized making it hard to recall the simplest things. As a "Sluggish Thinker", people who have sustained TBI will need to take extra care to move thoughts around quickly and cap them off for completion.

My Fall to Grace (A True Story)

In each chapter, I want to connect a real-life situation that I have gone through, to what you the reader, may have also gone through. I want you to come back and buy all of my books, so you can also learn how to be a better thinker for a better world.

Mid-Morning in February 2017, I had decided that I needed to get out of the house and go the gym. It was fairly pleasant, as far as the weather goes, but I just wanted to go to Tenacity Adventure Fitness, to walk on the treadmill and do some weight training.

We got to the facility and it was packed. There were no spots in the parking lot. "Let's go to the Gizzard Trail", I told my sons. I was already agitated because of working on something. I was fully involved in disaster thinking, and in my own habit of overthinking.

The Gizzard Trail, so you know, is a walking train called a day loop and the entirety of the loop was only 2-miles. I was convinced that I could make it without passing out. I had my phone loaded with music to walk with, but my brain was still thinking about the project I left behind when I decided to go to the gym that day. I was in my addiction to the habit of overthinking. My mind never really engaged in the hike.

Noticing there were big roots coming out of the ground, my middle son, who was walking behind me, said, "Watch out for those roots"! At that moment some hikers were coming behind me and I started to rush. I was rushing to get out of the way, trying to avoid hitting the roots, thinking of the project I left at the house – and it happened.

Within about 10-seconds, my right foot kicked a root and I started to fall. During the fall, I could feel energetic beings around me, like Angels and Guardians. It was surreal and out of body.

Joshua, my middle son, was in front of me. He heard me falling and turned around as if he were going to catch me. This meant he had a stance of strength and had his feet firmly planted on the ground. He is a strong man and could have caught me, but he was not close enough to me to prevent me from falling.

POP! The sound I heard when my forehead crashed into his knee, was loud; like a baseball cracking a homerun. Within 1-second I knew I had injured my brain and had to take care to get out of the trail. The fall resulted in a TBI and concussion. I had a knot the size of a baseball, on my forehead and my body started to turn cold.

Without thinking too much, I tightened my bandana on my forehead, and we started out of the trail. Through 1-mile of rocky, hilly, dangerous terrain, I managed to finally get back up to the parking lot. My message was clear: Take Care of Your Brain! I have sense moved back into my natural category of a "Genius Thinker", because I already had coping mechanisms stored in my memory.

The Self-Imposed Sluggish Thinkers

On the other hand, the "Sluggish Thinker" who has exposed his or her brain to consistent physical abuse by over consuming drugs or alcohol, may have killed off too many brain cells to evolve back into a better thinker, whether it's all the way to Genius or perhaps to General. The sluggish thinker in this area will need a lot of rehab the deep desire to be a better thinker and retrain their brain away from the addiction.

Sluggish thinkers due to substance abuse, are usually frustrated because they have not always been sluggish thinkers. Whatever condition they have allowed to consume their head space, has taken over any skills they may have had as previous types of thinkers. This would be like my sister, for example. She was a "Smart Thinker" because she was a certified public accountant. Her list of clients was amazing, and she had a Math-oriented brain.

She became addicted to pain medication and other abuses followed. I watched as her brain slowly deteriorated and heard her say that she just wasn't the person she once was. She tried to come out of it many times, and it drove her deeper into her drug addiction.

The Soulful Thinker

A soulful thinker thinks with their heart. They are thinking, but at the same time, they are very spiritual and have a lot of cloud moments. A soulful thinker can stay on a scholarly topic only for a few moments, before turning the thought into a spiritual moment. The communicate in color and are very creative.

The Smart Thinker

The Smart Thinker is keen on researching everything. They want to know the beginning, and the end, of any and all areas of concern. The smart thinker is never wrong, and thus often difficult to deal with.

However, this type of thinker can be found in our doctors, lawyers and educators.

Smart thinkers are hungry to be right. They insist on winning arguments and are often disciplined or ridiculed in work relationships for trying to overthink. While smart thinkers deeply think, many times they are not in the habit of overthinking because their need to researching and find solutions, is focused on the outcome and not the process.

Overthinking can happen to a smart thinker when they spend too much time in the information gathering process and miss deadlines or don't present a solution in a quantifiable amount of time. Smart thinkers must work toward taking aligned action toward a solution, at checkpoints along the path of being right.

As a Paralegal in 2005, I learned the strategic art of working with lawyers and judges to win Civil Litigation cases in court. I was both a researcher and a writer. My hunger to learn more, would have me up at all hours of the night, researching Westlaw (A Legal Research Emporium), tracking down cases at the state and Federal level to support the adjoining writing assignment that I was working on. However, in staying up all hours of the night, I quickly became lethargic and tired – which caused me to be less of a smart thinker and more of a non-thinker. There is a balance to everything.

As you are moving these lessons, you will find that you fit into one of these categories, most of the time. You will learn many things about who you are and what you expect out of life. As you become a better thinker, you will start to close feedback loops that don't serve you and learn how to create new neuro-pathways in your brain.

I learned so much during my time in the legal system, and those lessons are the foundation of why I have decided to write this book. See, for the past few years, I have been trapped between a soulful thinker and a non-thinker. Because of this entrapment, I have suffered. Because I didn't know how to map out the type of thinker I am, I didn't know how to navigate situations that seemed to challenge and trigger me. By challenge, I mean "Nearly Make Me Blow my Top", kind of challenge.

I am also a creative thinker and love the arts, music, fonts, beauty, colors and nature so I have to take time to nurture each one of my thought personalities to ensure maximum success and avoid the habit of overthinking in any area.

The Non-Thinker

These are the people who refuse to think about anything of importance, and spend their days in front of a television, playing a game, or glued to their cell phones. This type of thinker is usually an introvert or someone who suffers from a mental disorder, or fear of people.

A non-thinker will do their best to not have meaningful thought and will smother themselves in mindless activity. Have you ever been around someone who prefers to stuff their mind with television, the social media feed, or mindless television? The non-thinker prefers to be isolated from others, so they can engage in anti-thought, without risking being wrong. Social media and the bottomless quantity of viral vides of baby goats, jibber-jabber, and media blasphemy is developing a society of non-thinkers at an alarming rate.

Social media is the #1 culprit on our list of brainwashing tactics to convince people that they don't need to think. During the years between 2015 and 2018 I saw more children with cellphones that I did without them. I recall many times when the family would be out to dinner and an entire family (including mine) would have a phone in their hand.

The availability of apps and games, social networking and brain numbing activities has caused the number of non-thinkers to explode. There are more people today that start their morning with "Hey. I tagged you on a post" as the first words spoken, that there are people who are into the morning coffee, yoga and family talking.

When you are a smart thinker, a creative thinker or an innovative thinker and you are around a non-thinker, your tendency will be to lean toward their thought personality because you may be afraid that your creative thinking personality will be jeopardized, or will in some way, intimidate the non-thinker.

Determining your Thinking Personality

Personality A – You are a Genius Thinker and your life revolves around creating something new, or an idea to make something better. You are constantly looking for ways to improve the world.

Personality B – You are a sluggish thinker. You have brain fog often and find it hard to entertain thoughts with straight lines. Your thoughts will wonder around and you get frustrated easily. You may feel confused often and find it hard to deal with other people.

Personality C – You may not want to admit this, but you are someone who has used drugs or damaged your thought system in one way or the other. It's ok to classify yourself here, because we are going to work on helping you move into a different level of personality.

Personality D –

Personality E –

Neuro Lesson 3

No matter what type of thinker you are, it pays to have knowledge to add to your personality type. Innovative thinkers get caught in figuring it out, while non-thinkers simply veg out on mindless activity. This lesson is going to require some thought.

1. If you have classified yourself as a genius thinker, you are personality A. Your lesson is to engage in actions that a non-thinker would engage in. This will help you to get out of your feedback loop momentarily.
2. If you have classified yourself as a sluggish thinker due to a head injury or learning disability, please take a moment and try to invent something, anything, by researching it on the Internet and making a thesis of how it will benefit the world.

CHAPTER 4

5 Layers of Thinking

"We don't want you to stop thinking, we simply want to see you grow to become a productive thinker"

We could not call ourselves humans, if we didn't have thoughts. Thinking is necessary, but to be a good thinker we need to be aware of the different types of thoughts and their meaning. Just as we have looked at the 5 types of "Thinkers" we now are going to look at the 5 Types of "Thinking". You have heard the phrase "Thoughts become Things"? Perhaps you have heard "What you think about, you bring about?"

These are all phrases that related to a process of thinking a certain way. In the book "The Science of Getting Rich" by Wallace D. Wattles, the author says that if you want get Rich you must do things a certain way, and when you do things a certain way, you are bound to get rich. I have isolated 5-types of thinking to give you an idea.

The 5-Types of Thinking

Survival Thinking – Probably the most common of all thinking types, survival thinking stats with seeing a life that is minimalist, from paycheck to paycheck, with the chief focus being on providing just what is needed. 90% of humans live an existence based on Survival Thinking. This type of thinking has roots deeply planted into your subconscious, as well as woven in the fabric of your DNA. The thoughts you have about getting through life, all center around this type of thinking.

We find this type of thinking in financial transactions, marriages, parenting and dealing with sudden loss. It's perfectly ok to engage in survival thinking, but the trick is to tune into the survival thoughts that overcome productive thoughts and save the survival thoughts for when there is real danger and you must act quickly to save your life or the life of another.

This type of thinking shows up when the bills are due, if you get a flat tire or if you find out you are having a baby. This type of thinking shows up at the grocery store when you are comparing the price of name brand products, and generics. This type of thinking is with you always, every day.

Loose Cannon Thinking

Loose-cannon thinking is part of life. Loose cannon thinking is simply that; it's a mirage of thoughts with no solutions apparent. In the space of being addicted to barely thinking, this type of thinking frustrates others involved. These thoughts are the ones that come at you in the morning. As you are trying to do your morning ritual, meditate, reduce stress, plan the day, feed the kids, write in your journal, etc., these thoughts come to you like asteroids.

When you first wake up in the morning, you are in the loose-canon moment. This type of thinking is just your central control system trying to wake you up to what you need to do that day. You will find that this type of thinking fills your mind with fragments of thoughts that drive you nuts. Women, especially, are in this type of thinking, pretty much all day. They are chasing kids, paying bills, going to work, dealing with their own flood of ideas and trying to save the world.

The best way to tame this type of thinking is to plan the night before, what type of day you want to experience; before your head hits the pillow.

To break the habit of loose canon thinking, you must instill a new habit of 1-Thought. Your mantra "I fully accept and partially close, this 1 thought. Onward to the next thought".

Strategic Thinking

Strategic thinking can be akin to military planning in the War Room. When you are thinking of a strategy, you are in the mindset of a football coach. You are thinking about your moves, their moves and the end result. Loose cannon thinking enters occasionally, but for the most part, strategy thoughts are bulletized and clean. Obviously, strategy thinking can result in overthinking and may feel like you are in a video game that you can't escape from. If you have a strategy you need to create, its best to do it on paper. Writing something down, immediately brings you out of a thought, and into a solution.

Strategy can quickly turn into a military style plot. Your strategy may be flawed, or it may be successful. This type of thinking requires discipline to shift. As you are creating the strategy, you bring others into the thought panel. You may be creating a strategy for mitigating confusion for a group of people you are teaching. You may be creating a strategy for paying off bills. You may be creating a strategy for losing weight or getting healthier.

As you can see, strategy thinking is going to invoke other areas of life that can keep you in a feedback loop. If you are thinking of a strategy for mitigating confusion, you may be thinking about the many ways your group will be confused.

Logical Thinking

Unlike strategic thinking, logical thinking invokes your need to remember common sense knowledge that you have learned over your lifetime. Logic and reason, as you know, are the most common solutions to everyday challenges. Normal situations such as "Adding Detergent to the Laundry" are simple and logical thoughts. Overthinking in the logic space, starts a thought process within yourself on what should be the right solution to any problem. The problem with chronic logic thinking is that your beliefs get skewed over time and not revisited with your awareness.

Remembering what your parents or teachers taught you as a young child, starts the process of "Well. I am right." And this is the downfall of overthinking logic. You may have been taught by your parents that children should eat all of their food. They may have yelled at you for not eating all of your food. Your may believe this is the right way to parent, yet you see that your own children are obese, and they cry when they are forced to eat all of their food.

Logical thinking needs to be carefully examined because this is where you can change a generational belief. When you see that your logic is simply not making any sense in your own experience, you should work on noting the times when you are trapped in logical thinking and make the choice to change your belief.

Creative Thinking

Rainbows and unicorns, fairies and dragons – a creative thinker is always expanding a thought in living color. Creative thinkers don't stay in any thought long because they want to pull out the coloring sheets and draw something to represent their thoughts. Creative thinkers can create mind maps and strategies that are pretty. The problem with overthinking from the creative zone is that explaining a thought, as it a board meeting or to others, is difficult because creative thoughts are so personal to the creative thinker.

I am a creative thinker. If I have an IDEA, my intuition runs me straight to a hot pink backpack filled with markers of every style and color. I have over 1000 markers, some with gold and silver glitter, others that have the scent of fruit and chocolate. I have over 20 adult coloring books to release my creative genius, and this is where I thrive. Creative thinkers are always in "Living Color". A mind map can never be an Excel spreadsheet, but a colorful page of swirls, stars and drawings. Creating thinking is the essences of IDEA master, but it too can be cumbersome and here's why.

If you have not already noticed, you may do all of these types of thinking on a daily basis, and you interact with others who may be in one of the other types of thinking at any given time. As a creative thinker, when I interact with a linear or strategic thinker, I am often not heard nor understood, so I have to invoke with intention, another type of thinking so I can keep harmony in the unit. My passion is in activating human potential through my conversations, so mastering every type of thinking, and knowing when to switch, is something I have learned to do.

Creative thinking carries you through your imagination, all the way to a vision of what it is you want to manifest or bring into your world. Just like the other types of thinking, you can get trapped in the creative process, so you must learn how to take your creativity into strategy, using logic minimally. Try something new and see for yourself. Make a colored map of a dream you have, let it sink in. This is the best way to overcome the habit of overthinking.

Remember Thoughts Lead to Things and Attach to Emotions.

Understanding the Certain Way

Noted author Wallace D. Wattles, in *The Science of Getting Rich*, is clear when he says, "You will get rich with Mathematical Certainty, when you begin to do things a certain way". But he does not indicate what the certain way may look like. He only says there is a certain way. How then can you begin to think in a certain way, with this certain mix of thinking that creates the best results the fastest? How can you impactfully blend the different styles of thinking, with your thinking personality?

The way you think is connected to your thinking personality as well as the thought types listed in the next chapter. Knowing how to make fast decisions is one way to create your own certain way. Here are some situations where you may need to be observant to the different thinking types that pop up as you are trying to do your personal development work. Take note and practice shifting.

Visualizations Lead to Overthinking

Have you had success with lucid dreaming or intense visualization? I noticed recently that while in a visualization of something I want to manifest, I entered into the visual with massive overthinking. Before I knew it, I was trapped in the loop. As I visualized what the kitchen would look like in my new house, I started to think about how much the cabinets would cost. The next thing that happened is that renegade song started to play in my head.

Thinking in a Certain Way Out of Visual Loops

I was very deep into the process, so it took a lot of effort to come out of the overthinking process. Visioning is a very powerful tool for manifesting the life you desire but can end you up in a strong vortex of overthinking. Try taking your visualization time, when you can craft the visions you want, and you can know with certainty that the process is for your own mental manifesting, and not to figure out all of the details.

Meditating and Overthinking

Have you ever seen the movie Eat, Pray Love with Julia Roberts who is playing the author Liz Gilbert? She goes to an Ashram in India to learn more about herself. Part of the process was to spend a certain amount of time meditating. She is sitting there in meditation, and you can literally see the thought bubbles forming above her head. As she tried to clear her mind, she is thinking about building a meditation room in her house, and how the clock seemed to not be working fast enough.

Meditation is the best way to empty your brain of old thoughts but provides a fertile space for overthinking. Mantras are the key to humming your way through a period of no-thought during meditation. Deepak Chopra does a 21-Day Experience where he asks you to take 21-Days to work on meditating through a subject such as weight loss or finding your flow.

Clearly, when attempting to relax into non-thinking, thoughts will come flying at you. The central purpose of meditation is to clear your mind of fluttering old thoughts. Letting these thoughts leave your mind, frees up space for new patterns and pathways. Old patterns of overthinking, make no sense at all. Try doing meditations for about three minute each and go from there. Remember, the Yogis and Gurus have developed their whole life around the ability to meditate each day. Thoughts are things and things attach to emotional reactions, so incorporating this practice helps you become a better thinker, and fulfills the mission of this project.

Neuro-Lesson 4

Breaking the habit of overthinking starts with the type of thinking you have a habit of keeping. All 5 thinking types can go overboard. I want you to do this lesson in a span of 30 minutes, so you can see and feel how each type of thinking impacts your book and emotions.

1. When you are logically thinking, which other type of thinking comes into your mind?
2. When you are in loose-cannon thinking, what types of steps do you take, to get back into strategic or logical thinking?
3. Which thinking type gave you the most hope? Which type of thinking made you feel uneasy? Which two-types, do you feel you can combine most of the time?

Engaging your brain in various ways, helps create new pathways in your brain and helps you to be a better human.

CHAPTER 5

Protecting an Idea Like Your Very Life is Completely Depends on It!

The seed of an idea is found on cloudy days and on sunny days. This idea is meant only for you.

Have you ever had an idea that kept you up all night thinking about it? I love the story of Liz Gilbert's adventure with an idea in the book "Big Magic". She talks about an idea she had for a book that was about a couple who fell in love, and it was sort of a pirate book about Brazil. In the delightful non-fiction book, she absolutely validates the fact that an idea is presented to your awareness with the intention of being born through you. You are the incubator of an idea. When this idea comes to you, it will thump you on the ear, wake you up from the deepest sleep, and bother you until you turn your attention to it.

It is here where you have a couple of choices, and overthinking is one of those choices. Now, you can tell the idea to bug off and leave you alone, which will make it very sad. Or, you can start to allow the idea to branch out through you and grow, giving you joy and love; like a new boyfriend. Finally, you can make the totally stupid decision to overthink the idea, go looking to trademark the thought that has not left the undercurrent of your imagination, hire a coach, get a second, third or fourth opinion – you get my drift?

The habit of overthinking is chronic, and it is an idea killer and dream stealer. Once you make the decision to continue the addiction to your habit, you take the chance of losing money, giving up a potentially new life with more vacation, more leisure and more options. Your overthinking will crowd out the growth of ideas from your creativity cortex. (Known as Right Brain)

Shark Tank

Recently, my sons and I started watching the reality show Shark Tank, and one of the contestants "In the tank" had created a little novelty, stick on neck tie. So, the two women who were neighbors, came up with the idea to make a party favor that was a stick-on neck tie, to entertain children (and adults). Their idea got them all the way to production and into stores. They were doing well selling their product through the internet, and they made their pitch to the sharks.

Later on, in the show, 4 of the 5 sharks laughed the idea down the drain, said the valuation was too high, the sales were too low and the whole idea should be taken outside and shot. Low and behold, Mark Cuban offered to buy the whole business for $200,000. Now, let's start to see this as a lesson in over-thinking that killed a good idea. The two contestants cried and lamented at giving up their baby. They talked to each other on the side about how they would have more time with their kids if they sold the business, and they went on to accept the offer.

Since my two sons are addicted to the habit of overthinking, and the reason for this book to begin with, they started looking to see what happened to the business. Oh yea, I guess I should tell you that we were watching recorded episodes. Nickolas, my youngest son, was already Googling the company to see what became of the idea. It seems that, even though they accepted Mark's offer to buy the entire business, they ended up backing out because they felt guilting over selling the whole company.

Mark offered to be their advisor and help them build up the company to scale. Despite both offers, the business failed and went out of business. In the moment that these two women decided to overthink the process, they not only lost $200,000 but they lost their baby. The baby could have enjoyed a long ride with the Dallas Mavericks Basketball team, but instead, wound up in the garage.

Overthinking is the arch enemy of innovation. If you have an idea, protect it with your life. This book is the result of an idea that I had after banging my head on the wall with people who I was trying to sell a product or service to, who could not afford $50. They had to think about the time commitments, the money commitments and the energy required. They had to think about everything under the sun. How the planets aligned, and the moon moved in the sky.

Intuitive Decisive Empowered Action ™

In one of my renegade branding experiences, I created a program called the Idea Mastery System. It was designed to help people master their ideas. I came up with an acronym: Intuitive Decisive Empowered Action. IDEA! When an idea comes to you, it often creeps in unexpected and triggers your reaction system. Remember, your reaction system is more of a metaphysical and unique representation of what exists in the subconscious mind.

When an idea comes to you, automatically you begin to play in your own habit of overthinking. *The Idea Mastery System* was focused on ways to release the idea through writing and action. Little did I know, that in creating the Idea Mastery System, I was actually preparing to write this book about chronic over thinking. So, how can you master your ideas, so you don't get wound up in endless feedback loops of doubt or excessive over-analysis? **I will be mentioning this system**

and philosophy throughout the book, so you may see it more than once.

First let's look at the potential of a single idea and find some historic case-studies along the way. I will start. Ideas visit me every minute of the day. When I get an idea, the first thing I do is buy the domain name. That's right. I go to Godaddy.com and purchase the closest domain name to my idea. I take fast, aligned action sooner when an idea makes my heart race. But, ideas need protecting.

When I was married to my trial husband, Troy, the father of my two sons Joshua and Nickolas, we found our greatest bond to be talking about ways to improve something or to invent something that no one has ever considered. Literally, we would talk until the sun came up, just piddling around with ideas for new inventions.

"What if we invent a washer/drier combo that was one piece", I said to him late one night. My idea was that there should be one unit that could wash the clothes, then turn into a drier so the process was seamless. We drew out the diagrams, created the process of how the machine would work, and we sent it to the Inventers Program to see what they said. In a split second our idea was lost. Why? Because once there, they send you this amazing welcome letter tell you that your idea is patent worthy, then direct you to the $10,000 price tag to get started. The Idea was there, but the due-diligence was not there.

Within the year, we saw our idea in the Daymark Catalogue where someone had invented the system exactly as we had drawn it out. Because we didn't know what "aligned action" looked like, we probably lost over a million dollars in future money.

The Ideas you have in your mind, are living entities, capable of making money. But, your habit of overthinking, could shove them out the door. Each time you have an idea, the trick to mastering it, is to write it down, research it then to end the thought then determine what the next best action will be. Don't try to map out a 12-month marketing strategy, just move from thought to thought, acting quickly along the way.

To master anything, you must practice that thing until the process is natural.

I developed the framework for this system last year as I was overthinking and pondering on what I could create for the world. I thought of the people I had met and interacted with on social media, then I thought of what I did best. Every conversation I can recall having resulted in the person saying to me, "That is a great idea", then my own light bulb started to go off.

"What if I can teach people how to take that idea, even the ones I donated to them, and make something from it?", I asked myself.

I want to give you the short version of the Idea Mastery System, so you can be empowered to give birth to ideas you may have, even those that come to you in the dark hours of the night.

First, we need to do a little mindset work. Remember, when an idea comes to you, it will not feel normal. Your overthinking habit will kick in and you will need to intervene. Intervention when breaking and addiction will be hard and take some self-work on your part. Your mind has convinced itself to overthink ideas, while talking yourself out of action. In talking yourself out of action, you are enforcing indecision and inaction.

The Mind Controls the Money

Before we go into the Idea Mastery System Mini-Course, we are going to work on how you feel about the possibility of success. I am talking about success, where you earn millions of dollars from every idea. Where every idea you have turns into a book or a program that people want to buy. What is your mindset of success?

Ask yourself this question, "If my idea works, who will it help and support? If my idea generates millions of dollars, how will I use the money?" The answers to these questions will amaze you. You hold within you, the seeds of ideas that could change the world. Your habit of Chronic Overthinking has drowned the seeds, or dried them out, so you must do this step – so your ideas can sprout.

Mastering your IDEAS is centered around the ability to ACT fast when a hunch comes knocking and knowing your actions will lead to another possible solution, or problem, either way, you will need to be ready to jump from experience to experience, all the way. Analyzing the success of your fast choices and letting go of bad results. Rather than judging your idea and throwing it out the window at the first sign of a problem, why not keep moving forward until you reach gold.

A Story of the Little Seed that Became a Big Tree

Many of my books have focused on the invisible realm of growth and magic. I have written about the subconscious mind, the power of our thoughts to impact the manifestations we enjoy and attract, and our ability to heal our own bodies. I have mapped out family patterns and created a process for coming out of an emotional experience. And, all of my writings talk about a seed.

Your beliefs about success and failure, are not surface level issues that can be thought away, they must be changed with intention. Your belief about succeeding or failing, is important as you decide to break the habit of overthinking, and as you practice jumping. So, let's talk just for a moment about the seed that became a big tree.

Stop just for a moment and get ready to do some creative thinking. I want you to go back to the chapter on different types of thinking.

Now, visualization is part of the creative process, so you are going to take a moment to intentionally visualize the inside of a seed. This may take some practice. When you see an acorn, which is a seed, you may see some type of nut that falls on the ground, but inside of the acorn, there is a code of instructions that helps the seed burst forth, connect to the earth and start the process of becoming a tree.

Your idea is an acorn.

As the seed gets more nutrients, it starts to grow little branches and will just look like a plant. Each year, with support of the sun, water and warmth, the sprout gets bigger until a full tree is the result. From the tree, more acorns. From more acorns, more trees and the tree now is fully independent and can continue the process of reproduction.

An idea is like a seed. Once you start the process of nurturing the idea, you start the process of something that will be there for you a lifetime. In business, a product that is created once, and continues to provide value, is called evergreen. There is no wonder why this word was chosen, because an evergreen tree, grows all year long, providing oxygen to the planet, just as a once created product, provides income to the producer (YOU).

As we go to our next lesson, get ready to unleash your ideas and watch them grow.

Neuro-Lesson 5

Getting in tune with the natural rhythm that requires no thought, but by default, is perfection at its finest. This lesson requires you to get dirty, as in planting a seed.

The seed has instructions but no thought, yet it blooms in its wonder when the conditions are right. For this lesson, we are going to plan an imaginary seed and a real seed.

- Get about 1 cup of potting soil and a seeding kit. Do this indoors. Plant any variety of seed and write down your feelings on what this seed will produce, how you will use the plant, and your thoughts on the process. When the seed begins to sprout, give it even more attention.
- Step Two – The Seed of Your Creation. Now that you have explored how to generate and nurture and idea, I want you to write in your journal, the types of seeds you are planting and how they will grow. Remember to end any thought that goes too far and replace it with a solution.
- Finally, write in your journal, the experience you had as you were doing the lessons above. Did it make you think more, think less or think balanced?

CHAPTER 6

Learning to Become a Jedi Master of Idea Generation and Action

"You must burn all bridges of doubt if you are to become a master of the IDEA and keep your eyes forward"

After reading Big Magic by Liz Gilbert, I began to truly think about, what it meant to be an idea incubator, wondering just where the hell ideas came from. In my last book The Totality of Everything Philosophy, I talk about moving through experiences by bending and being resilient to life's challenges. The more I started to embrace the definition or identity behind an idea, the more it became clear that the idea inside of your mind, keeping you up at night, was put there by a source you may never see or understand. It is, however, inside of you so you will take action to give birth to it.

Every great inventor, started out with an idea. Now, the topic of being a Jedi Master of the Idea, ties directly into the title of this book "Breaking the Habit of Overthinking" because an idea, when fully activated, usually grows from some swift action to bring it to life.

When an idea appears to you as a hunch, or a flutter in your belly, that is a sign to take an action. In the chapter 5 we talked about an idea being like an acorn, and the new sprouts growing into a tree. I wanted you to do some creative thinking to see that your ideas, can turn into profit, when nurtured. But, you must take action and do it quicker, rather than researching it longer. There is no one right way of being a Jedi Master of your Ideas.

Action is Moving and Flowing

Taking an action could be as simple as writing your idea on paper, or as complex and filing for a patent. But, action must be taken. If you put away the idea until another day, if you deliberate on its worth, you are telling it to take a hike. Millions of dollars have been lost from people who stopped 1 inch from gold. So, you must become a good steward of any idea that is living within your paradigm.

When "The Idea Mastery System" came to me in a vision, I thought for hours on what it was that I actually taught people from day to day. I wanted to ping my niche. My own thoughts began to recall memories of conversations with others, then my thoughts would start to churn up emotions. Why? In my making of many mistakes, I failed to take action on my ideas, but through my conversations with others, I found I was giving away ideas. Other people were taking my ideas and running with them.

What is an Idea?

From a logical stand point, it seems that we create ideas, but if you have ever had a really big one, you know that they seem to come to you by magic, in the middle of the night, during a hardship or while engaged in an activity. Overthinking is an idea stealer and dream killer. Remember, your job is NOT to stop thinking, but to be a better thinker. Your job is not to eliminate all thoughts with any possibility of negative outcome, but to see the positive outcome sooner.

To be an idea master, you must learn to act faster when you feel an idea come to you. The IDEA is yours and yours alone, placed there from somewhere (The Universe). Capture an idea. Move on it. Done.

The Idea Mastery System ™ is a process where you feel the idea, write it down, research the potential and make a choice. Your idea could improve the world, if fully born, and your idea may just be the seed that grows another idea. Either way, when an IDEA is present, you must not be in the habit of overthinking.

Great inventors all suffered from overthinking at one point in their journey. They may have over thought a process or system, while the idea of the invention slowly left their consciousness. Maybe they worried too much about the idea failing, being looked at negatively, or wasting time. Most likely, one of the self-defeating thoughts was centered around money, not having enough to make it happen, or not seeing a return on investment.

Mark Zuckerberg had an idea. His idea was to start a portal where college students could communicate with each other without going to a meeting. His idea is now the foundation of Facebook, with over 2-Billion users who log in over a billion times each day. No matter where you go, someone is saying the word Facebook. This idea was planted into the world as a way to communicate, and the world responded. No one would have predicted the success of Facebook, but Z had to take action on his idea, then it became a burning desire.

Since Facebook's humble beginnings, the world now connects through the massive social media platform to expand their ability to work in virtual communities, globally, for free. See how many problems Facebook solved for the masses? This can be your idea too. Your idea is just as worthy as his was and can be just as lucrative if you tap into a need.

Being a Masterful Master at Mastery

Thoughts are there for a reason, and ideas are there for a season. Just as Mark, Steve and Bill all had ideas that blossomed into massive money, your ideas are just as potent. They are there to serve you as you serve them. My acronym for IDEA – Inspired Decisive Empowered action. When you have an idea, you are inspired. By being decisive, you have pre-planned your strategy for birthing the IDEA. The empowerment comes when you decide to ACT on the idea by researching it and writing it in your IDEA Manifesto.

Poverty is a condition of the mind. It's a fear of there never being enough, and a deeper fear of impending doom and loss. Because part of my personal vision is to see a world, void of the poverty brain, it's important that I show you how to always get yourself out of a poverty mindset. Helping you see your ideas as valid, creates a new money path in your brain, and shows you that you can think your way out of poverty. As with all of our lessons, this chapter will end with an assignment for you, in how to recognize a poverty thought.

Your ideas are worth money. Every time you allow an idea to pass through you and you don't take aligned action, you are saying that you wish you stay in the thought process of poverty. Overthinking a prosperity-based idea, can put your brain back into the poverty feedback loop.

Since I hang out with 1000's of people online, I know that the first thought that pops up into their minds when I say to them something like "Wow, you can invent a widget, and make lots of money with it". Their feeble reply for the most part is "Oh, I don't need a lot of money, just enough to get by." With these words, the reality is created.

The thought processes surrounding poverty, touch everything that could result in money because it's easier to churn up thoughts about lack than it is to venture the thoughts into the arena of riches or prosperity. I have to get past the poverty thought process many times, every day, to be able to gather confidence in myself. Money is not the only lack thought inside of the brain, but nearly every other area of life has been touched by the word money.

Document Scanning

In 2006, there was enacted a new set of laws pertaining to attorneys and discovery material, which turned the industry on its head. The legal system has always been paper-based, with buildings filled with copies of legal documents and discovery items. You may know this.

I was an eager paralegal in 2006 when I overheard my boss complaining that the filing system was going electronic by the end of the year. In Alabama, you can imagine that this news started a panic. Not only were they not equipped, but staff was not really educated on the process.

Light Bulb

My thoughts began to race as the idea came to me. I was so excited that I could hardly wait to learn how to implement my idea. I took action and spoke with one of my college professors about the feasibility of doing remote scanning for law firms and charging by the page to scan the discovery documents, then creating an index on Excel that was clickable, so they could retrieve the documents quickly in trail or discovery. I researched portable scanners and found one for $1400.00. As soon as my tax refund came that year, I purchased the scanner and started looking for prospective jobs.

Within a week I had secured a contract with a large legal firm to scan 2500 document over a 2-week period of time. I charged them .50 cents per page to cover the time for creating the Index document. That was a $5,000 job. The same company retained me 2 more times for the same type of work. Within 5 months I had earned $20,000 just from acting on the idea.

Of course, it didn't take long before offices became equipped with the appropriate scanning systems, and the window of my success from action on the idea, was narrow. The point is that I took it. The possibilities of success, far outweighed the thought of failure. This was one of my greatest ideas.

To be a master of your IDEA you have to take fearless action and decide to not overthink. There are no statistics out there to measure something that has yet to be created. From shoestrings, to tiny computer processors, to satellite signals, to a new flavor of coffee – you cannot know the reasons for success and failure of an idea that lives only in your brain.

Intuition is the Counter Balance of Thought

Thoughts are in your mind and feedback loops, hidden in the folds of the human brain. They are dominant during any given day. Intuition, the counter part of your bodies control system, is just a mixed back of hunches, that trickles into your though system. For women, intuition is a major player in their ability to act on ideas, but it can be confused with other less attractive situations such as anxiety or depression. You must, and I repeat, you must, learn to distinguish intuition from mental imbalance. It is no such thing. Intuition is there for you for your survival and to thump you on the head when an IDEA is gestating. So, don't run out to the doctor every time you feel a little nudge

If you are sitting at the school, waiting to pick up your kids, and think, "I feel like something is wrong", it probably is. If you are coming to an intersection and something says, "Turn here", and you don't, you may find yourself in an unfortunate car accident. If your million-dollar idea, nudges you and the feeling is the same, listen to it.

Simply say, "Wow. I am going to make it happen." Your inclination will be to quickly move to another thought, turn on the radio, or pick up your cell phone. You have to pre-pave the process by declaring now, that you are the master of the IDEA and your mastery skills are Jedi worthy. There are so many success stories of good ideas turning into crazy profit.

Several times, I have referenced Shark Tank because it's amazing to me to see so many "youthpreneurs" put their ideas in front of the sharks, with hopes and dreams as big as the Universe. Many of their ideas, go on to be products and successful businesses solving massive problems for the world, while others get sent home in disappointment. The fact is, they took action on an idea and burned all bridges behind them on the way.

Henry Ford (Add More Research)

Think and Grow Rich by Napoleon Hill talks about how Henry Ford persisted with his idea, even in the face of a community ready to arrest him. He kept on until the concept became real, and now there are automobiles that run off of electricity by plugging into an outlet. Where would the world be now, if Henry Ford had of said, "Nope. Too Hard. I Quit". Rather than over thinking, he moved into imperfect action to make his dream a reality.

Playing the Virtual Business Game

As you can see by now, I am an Author. I started on Facebook by doing marketing as a web designer way back when Geocities was the only way an individual could have a website. I joined what was called "Web Rings", meaning a circuit of websites on a certain topic. I watched Google become a search engine and have followed the virtual platform since then.

An Entrepreneur Cannot Succeed at all – if they remain in the habit of overthinking for more than a week, when wanting to launch something in the Virtual Space, because technology changes just that fast. Google is a perfect example. When the search engine giant first started its indexing service, it was much like a digital library. If you wanted to learn about something, you could type in keywords and a website would come up as a result based on the keyword you put in. There were only a few websites in existence at that time.

The dawn of this technology started to wake up the brains of digital pioneers all over the world. The ideas could almost be seen in the sky.

They were thinking of unique ways to hack the system, bring their own websites to the top based on keywords, and take advantage of various inlets to the search engine.

Google responded by shifting its algorithm every time the wind blew, so the search results were meaningful. For a time, you could buy top space from Google based on your company keywords, etc. and again, idea masters from the dark side, infiltrated the feature so that paid ads came on top, but the actual importance of the result was not there.

Today, Google is a voice commanded search engine, primarily, and is centered around serving a variety of results based on natural language input. So, had I not kept abreast of this, I would have been in the dark. Google is still my preferred search engine, although others are trying to compete. I know the company value system and believe they are always trying to make life much easier through intuitive results. Example: Navigate Home. This is a command you can give Google and it will pull up a navigation map and start to give you voice directions to the place you call home, on your phone. Very interesting.

Pioneers are still needed. Those brave enough to see the future, and believe something will happen, well before it does, will reap the rewards of money from acting on thoughts that produce ideas. Facebook now has over 2 billion members. Will Facebook remain as a social media giant, or will it flop on its face?

Neuro-Lesson 6

Create your future product or solution today by using your brain to think of one thing you could create from an IDEA, that would serve the world and create money for your life.

1. I had an idea about _____ and I am ready to take aligned action toward bringing this idea into the world.
2. This idea would help the _____ with problems such as _____.
3. I will research the possible benefits and write my thoughts on the results in my Neuro-Journal within 12 hours of completing the research. I will look for:
    a. The possibility of people buying this service.
    b. The possibility of a grant to build this product.
    c. The possible competition.
4. I will assess my own feelings of success and carefully react accordingly, not getting caught in an overthinking feedback loop.

CHAPTER 7

The Neuroscience of a Thought Process and Endless Feedback Loops

"The brain is a monstrous, beautiful mess. Its billions of nerve cells - called neurons - lie in a tangled web that displays cognitive powers far exceeding any of the silicon machines we have built to mimic it."

- William F. Allman, Science Writer

When I decided to write this book, I had no idea where the idea came from. I had not thought the idea, nor pondered on it at all. When I had this idea, I took action.

When you think about a thought, and how one thought creates another thought, and so on – you must be aware that these thoughts are all created and processed in the brain. The neuroscience of a thought process dives deeply into the topic of feedback loops and what causes them. Overthinking is a habit. We have allowed a feedback loop to keep repeating itself. From life patterns, to anxiety, overthinking can be noted as a culprit; this is the neuroscience of a thought.

Let's explore this a little deeper, shall we? You know that your brain is the sending and receiving unit of your entire system. You know that your brain can work all the time, and it can work hardly ever. Your brain also is the storage area that contains your memories, reactions, responses and programming from your DNA. Thinking begins in the brain and touches all areas of what is stored inside your brain. Thoughts can be changed through intentional input of a different thought. When thought comes and feels negative, go immediately to the other end of the spectrum and say the opposite, then get out of the thought.

An emotional memory, for example, can be remembered more easily, without issue. This is why we are prone to clearly remember trauma, or joy, but are sluggish to remember the "in between". What we put into our brain is so very critical.

Storage is the passive process of retaining information in the brain, whether in the sensory memory, the short-term memory or the more permanent long-term memory. Each of these different stages of human memory function as a sort of filter that helps to protect us from the flood of information that confront us on a daily basis, avoiding an overload of information and helping to keep us sane. The more the information is repeated or used, the more likely it is to be retained in long-term memory (which is why, for example, studying helps people to perform better on tests).

The Habit of Overthinking, therefore, will cause the memory storage to be dominated by the thoughts that are consuming your

time and space. When a thinking process on one subject, lingers without a definite purpose or solution, it leaves behind a breadcrumb trail of confusion and unsettled thinking. If our brain is a storage unit, then it just makes good common sense, to Break the Habit of Overthinking, by replacing it with a new habit of "Quick Thinking" and "Quick Action". If you want to succeed in any area of life, you must master the art of being a better thinker, understanding what thoughts actually are, within your own brain.

It's truly interesting in many ways, that our brains can story unlimited memories, infinitely unless trauma occurs. If this is the case, then every human being needs to focus on putting in all of the good memories possible.

The indications are that, in the absence of disorders due to trauma or neurological disease, the human brain has the capacity to store almost unlimited amounts of information indefinitely. Forgetting, therefore, is more likely to be result from incorrectly or incompletely encoded memories, and/or problems with the recall/retrieval process. It is a common experience that we may try to remember something one time and fail, but then remember that same item later. The information is therefore clearly still there in storage, but there may have been some kind of a mismatch between retrieval cues and the original encoding of the information. "Lost" memories recalled with the aid of psychotherapy or hypnosis are other examples supporting this idea, although it is difficult to be sure that such memories are real and not implanted by the treatment.

The Habit of Overthinking and Memory Transmutation

Inside of the brain, the memories live. What is there, impacts your ability to be a better thinker, and create better thoughts and new habits. I totally understand how memories can impact your reality, both emotionally and physically. When you start to implant new habits into your brain, the thoughts that get you stuck, are generally attached to an emotion, which is attached to a memory.

In my first book, The Rock Bottom Chronicles, I give you a clean process for memory transmutation that allows you to bring up memories and change them at the level of the unconscious, so you will not have to deal with them. The clearer your nuero-pathways are, the easier it will be for you to learn new methods of thinking, while you let go of the habit of time-draining, overthinking.

Neuro Lesson 7

To effectively change habits that are associated with memories, you must take action toward replacing the memories with new ones and dealing with the less-than-happy ones. Don't worry, it's not as hard as your habit of overthinking might imply.

In your Neuro-Journal, start a section and name it "Memory Cleansing", this will get you all setup for the mindset work involved. Now, answer these three questions in your journal, and repeat every time a bad memory comes to you and a good memory comes to you.

1. The most horrible feeling memory I hold in my brain involves the time when I _____.
2. I choose to change this memory by being in the memory and shifting the part where _____.
3. Now that I have loved and cleansed the memory, I replace it with the best memory I have regarding the same situation which was _____.

Closing Mantra: I choose to re-remember things that caused me pain – as a situation that brought me to where I am today, thus forgiving the memory and clearing space for new thoughts and emotions. So it is.

CHAPTER 8

Using Common Sense to Decide when the Thought Can End

Common sense, is often disregarded as not-important, but it's there for you to use when you need to end a thought that goes on forever. Just say "This thought can end now", and be done with it"

As human beings we are constantly having thoughts and those thoughts continue until something happens to break the thought and causes the thought to end. For example, I recently have become hyper-aware of thought patterns that have repeated in my life, not for minutes or even days, but for years. In noticing these thought patterns, because of my decision to become hyper-aware of their contents, I realized that I was in a negative feedback loop trap with certain thoughts I had allowed to stay in my mind. These thoughts, as I observed within my own body, were the exact same, year after year.

Common sense is simply tapping into your intuition and acting on what you know, for the most part. When we begin to use this faculty more, we can end old thought patterns faster. I was caught in a feedback loop.

Because of their presence in my paradigm, no new thoughts could enter into my awareness. In blocking out the new thoughts that could consume the same space, I created more blocks to creating something fresh and fruitful. Overthinking is often not conscious thinking, but unconscious thoughts that are inside of your mind, rent free. Breaking this habit, has been hard for me. I have never been an alcoholic but imagine that detoxing from beer might be less hard, than breaking a thought pattern that is causing harm to my life. Choosing to end a thought is choosing to disrupt a pattern of thoughts.

In my book "The Soul Code: Activating the Secret to Living in Totality", I give the readers several lessons on pattern disruption, so they can understand what thought patterns are, and why they stick around for, so long. Pattern coherence is a skill you can develop when you run into repeating screen plays in life. Noticing that you are repeating patterns that are uncomfortable is your sign to invoke and engage in your own common sense.

Common sense is a skill you develop over time, when you just know things from their outward and instant appearance. Using common sense when confronted with something that feels negative and is obviously repeating over and over in your experience, starts with the lightbulb moment. It's really comical when you master the process of stepping back and looking at the situation that is repeating as a pattern in your journey.

The Internal Revenue Service

I want to paint a picture for you, of the "lightbulb moment" I had, just before sitting down to write this chapter. Be prepared to see yourself in this story and laugh with me as we dislodge the same pattern, from the walls of your mind. After all, every thought and every pattern, lives inside of your mind.

Since I am one of those people who has created a life where scarcity and lack (two thought patterns) were allowed to stay in my mind with no rent, every year at "tax time", I have fallen prey to the worry and anxiety that comes along with waiting for a refund. Being born in the state of Alabama, I have fortunately (or unfortunately) been in the income bracket where refunds were large. And, since I have three children, an IRS refund could be at any time, between $3000 and $10,000. That is a hefty amount of money to receive at once. You see that thought pattern and belief that I just now typed. "That is a pretty heft amount of money to receive at once". This is a clear indicator that I have been trapped in a thought pattern or two, and these patterns have mutated inside of me.

We are currently in the month of February, and I have sent off my tax return. The first thing that I do is to wait for the IRS to accept the return electronically. The second thing I do is start watching a stupid Facebook group called "Where's my refund?", where 1000's of people of little or no education, are rapping their woe's, wondering why their orange bars have disappeared. In playing there, I get a migraine. And, I go into the exact same worry.

This year, the IRS said that there would be an update on February 17, 2018 (which is the exact day I am typing this). I woke up, reached to grab my phone from the nightstand, hurting my eyes with the blue light in my face – only to see this "Your tax return is still being processed"!

Like fireworks, my neuro-path, well memorized, responds with stress. My brain starts to think about all of the things that possibly could be wrong with my return, keeping me from the glamorous refund that is staring at me. The amount of $3780 is out there waiting for me. They are keeping me from my refund. What is wrong? Do I need to call? Did I do something wrong? OMG I can't get the money right now! Are you laughing yet? If you have ever been waiting for a tax refund, I would bet you have gone through the same thing. So, you can thank me later.

Moving along, I said that to say this. Common sense helped me to step back and laugh. "I did this last year and the year before and the year before and the year before". Oh, and "I did this the year before that". I laughed and looked at the thought pattern as if it were an ex-lover and proclaimed the shift "Oh Hell No!", you are not paying rent in my mind and you are not allowed here. Glory!

In my last book "How to Bend the YOUniverse: Feeling Totality Through the Experience" I talk about how to move your emotions out of a negative "feeling" experience in my signature 3-Step Process where the first step is naming the experience, the 2nd is claiming the lesson and the 3rd is proclaiming the shift. The "Shift" is a snap point of your brain that says the feedback loop has ended, and you are going to focus your attention on new experiences. The moral of the story is this: When you don't seek out old thought patterns, they will nag at your being until you have healed them.

Getting out of an Old Thought

Your common-sense faculty will come to the rescue when you intentionally engage it as you are finding yourself in and out of positive and negative experiences. Just like my 3-Step program works to bring you quickly out of negative emotions, the common-sense process will get you out of long thoughts that result in no solution.

What is Common Sense?

Common Sense is that part of you which knows the truth and reality of the thought process. So, say you are in a thought process about which brand of milk to buy at the grocery store, and you are wondering if there is an inherent difference between the name-brand, and the store-brand. The store-brand is $2 less expensive than the name-brand, but there must be some difference, right? What could it be, this difference I feel? Is it the process, is it the age of the milk? What is the reason I should switch to the store-brand even though I have been buying the name-brand my entire life?

Now here is where you need the Common-Sense thump on the forehead. Why? There is a good chance that both brands are the same milk, and that the price is simply that, the lower price. Now you can pick up the gallon of milk with the lowest price and feel confident about your choice. Sometimes, there simply is not an answer that logical thinking will reveal, and your strategy of thought, will be for naught.

Act Fast and Move Along

I am very intrigued with the teachings of Mel Robbins, bestselling author of the 5-Second Rule and her method that asks you to count backwards from five and then take action. There is a sound reasoning behind what she teaches, and it is that your body gives you a clue and within the clue there is an associated action. If you slip out of the rule and start to overthink, you go into the stress mode that keeps you very stuck.

Being super stuck in a thought, hinders you from moving forward in any capacity and this is applicable to home life, parenting and careers.

When you make a choice faster, take aligned action and apply your knowledge, you are able to get to the solution much faster. When you get to the solution much faster, you can move to the next life experience and start to solve even more problems.

The Science of Decisiveness

To be Decisive is to be certain and to make definite decisions about important areas of life such as leading a team of workers at a factory or being the lead investigator of a crime. You must make it a priority to become more decisive in all you do. When you have knowledge, then you apply it with assertiveness, your goals will be reached far faster than if you simply think and think about what to decide.

In fact, overthinking can destroy a group who may be depending on your leadership. Make it a priority to stop the habit of overthinking so you can be a better human.

Neuro-Lesson 8

In this lesson you are asked to make fast decisions for 7-Days. This is going to be hard for you. Let's use Mel Robbins method for this lesson and learn to count down from five whenever you have a tough conflict to respond to in your day to day walk.

- When you need to make a decision about your family, say the problem out loud then count backward from five. When you get to zero, proclaim the decision. Your brain only needs 5-seconds to be able to make the right decision.
- When you need to make a decision about money, say the money issue out loud, then count backward from five. When you get to zero, say out loud, the choice you made.

What were your observations?

_____
_____
_____

CHAPTER 9

Healing Your Body by Breaking the Habit of Overthinking

Cortisol, Adrenaline and Sickness can all be triggered and tossed into Imbalance when thoughts stay around unresolved.

I recently watched a video on YouTube about the adrenal gland and cortisol. The relationship between staying in a thought too long, and the reactions available to the body from the branches of a thought, is this: If a thought is negative, it will result in your body reacting to the negative state of the thought. Example: You are very mad at someone and you start to think about why you are mad, this thought is going downward swiftly. Your body reacts to this thought. Your heart begins to beat faster, and cortisol triggers the survival mechanism.

In your moment of being stuck in a negative thought, you are creating a disease within your physical body. Why would you do this? Well, it's not at all uncommon when you are stuck in the addictive habit of chronic over thinking. Negative thoughts attach to negative emotions, which trigger the subconscious to release to you, all the reactions that it has stored. Breaking the habit of overthinking as it relates to your wanting to be healthier, starts with your awareness of thoughts that are very negative. You also must be ready to admit you have these thoughts and creating certain stop points, when you see you are in a negative thought pattern. It's very easy to take a single negative thought and turn it into a full-blown conversation inside of your own mind, that leads to zero solutions. One thought turns into a self-imposed battle with nobody but yourself.

I have engaged in self-sabotaging thoughts and am very guilty of starting a thought about someone who has done something I have considered to be wrong toward me. Before I know it, I take a single, renegade thought and turn it into tears, sadness, eye infections, the flu, aching legs, an aching heart and so on.

> "Thoughts need to come and go, ebb and flow. When they stick, they make you sick"

The Reality of Stress

Maybe you have read a million times that stress is not good for you, been told to meditate, or asked to tell a group what type of stress you are experiencing. While I agree, we all need a map from which to navigate the universe of imbalances within our mind and body, I disagree with the vagueness of most assessments of stress, and many of the possible fixes given by doctors and coaches.

When someone sees that you are sick, maybe you have come down with a cold, or have excessive tiredness, they may say to you, "Oh, it's probably stress." You usually reply, "That is probably right". At the mere mention of the word stress your body reacts and pulls out of its storage bank, any word association you feel with the term stress. Maybe it brings back the last day you went to work, or a painful memory. Whatever it does, the word stress has deep and powerful associations with many health-related issues.

At present I am recovering from an allergic reaction I had to a shampoo I used which literally burned my scalp. It put three spots on my scalp that were raw and got infected. I allowed the stress of this to bring me down so badly that I developed a swollen lymph node. The swollen node, put me into fear and panic because of the fear of cancer. This is what stress does to the body, and overthinking is probably one of the worse feeders of stress. Being caught in all of the what ifs, is so destructive to your body. The Brain begins to take what you fear, and attempt to make it real.

The habit of overthinking is chronic, and overthinking will cause stress in the form of worry. Now let's get a little scientific here. As mentioned able, cortisol is what has been named the "Stress Hormone". Our bodies are made to react to situations where we must protect ourselves and to survive. In this need to survive, the body switches to its default mechanism when stressful events are present.

Our emotional body is protected by the release of certain hormones during times of real and imminent danger.

When your system thinks that it is about to be attacked for real, or from the invisible plane, it releases these stress hormones. Although, cortisol serves a purpose, it's there for times of danger that are short-lived. In today's society, however, we stay in stress by default. This means that on any average day, nearly all of our thoughts can turn into stress in the blink of an eye.

Thinking is a brain activator, thus being in a thought, has the possibility of creating stress. Stress from not knowing what to do, stress from indecisiveness and stress from possible negative outcomes. You can feel stress from being in the thought, stress from not being able to connect the millions of loose thoughts in your mind, and stress from every memory a single thought can conjure.

When I am stuck in a repeating pattern of thinking, I find that my mind starts to create a play. I am in a theatre and all of the actors are around me. After a few minutes of being in a renegade thought, I am having conversations with the people who are in my presentation. Normally, I will be in an argument with the invisible people in my mind, about how I am right, and they are wrong.

The inner argument will continue until I intentionally stop the thought with my conscious mind, and clear instructions or I will start to get sick and even cry. I can trigger all of the emotions associated with the long thought, if I stay in the thought long enough.

Here you can clearly see how the habit of chronic overthinking, can lead to a physical response. Sadness is an emotion that attaches to memories of a loved one, so being in a thought long enough, can bring up the emotion from situations involving those you love the most. Before you even know it, this thought can create a sense of anguish to someone who, just 5-minutes prior, was not even on your mind.

Be Mindful of Inner Dialogue

This one trick will help you in protecting your physical core when you tend to be trapped in overthinking. The conversations in your head are invoked when you are overthinking, and they love to mess you up – like – literally. Every day you will have these conversations. Just like a Defense attorney will script and practice the Defense for court, you will always be preparing your defensive statement, inside of your mind.

Certain mental conversations focus on the "Gotcha" conversation. This is one where you are always finding the ace in your pocket and going over everything that could go wrong. You will be focusing on everything that can go wrong, and everything will go wrong. That's just the Law of Attraction in Action.

Neuro-Lesson 9

Powerful Affirmations Using the Tapping Technique. Tapping is a very successful method of moving energy through your meridians, including left over remnants of stress related events. You will need to be ready to release emotions as you release the times when you have been trapped in stressful overthinking.

Tapping is when you use the two fingers of one hand, to tap on various parts of your body. To start we will tap on our opposite hand, the top of our heads, our eyebrows, under our eye, and our chin. While tapping these meridians say the following three times.

1. I allow this stress to leave me.
2. I am 100% healed of stress.
3. I allow nice things to flow into my experience.
4. I allow positive situations to flow to me.

This is just a starting point. There are many affirmations to use with tapping for a physical and emotional release of overthinking.

Final Assessment

As you have wrapped up this short book about breaking the habit of overthinking, I leave you with these final words and this final lesson. You have done amazing. You can't stop thinking but you can learn to become a better thinker. You have discovered your thinking personality and have recognized specific patterns that have caused you stress. Now, this is the time when you make a promise to yourself. Here is the creed to break the habit of overthinking.

I will be observant to times when I seem to get caught in thought. I promise to take swift action when an idea comes to me and to take a quick 5-Second pause. By taking action faster, I allow the next experience to come to me for processing. I am creating new habits of thinking better and acting quicker so I can react and respond to important issues that require my leadership.

CONCLUSION

On 3/22, my granddaughter's birthday, I endured a great tragedy when my nephew pulled a gun and killed my sister's fiancé. I just had experienced an amazing day with my grandson, my granddaughters and my son and daughter in law. When we arrived back home from the birthday party of my middle grandchild, we got a call from my mother telling me of the tragedy. Immediately the habit of overthinking kicked into high gear and nearly made me faint.

As you can imagine, I was running every possible scenario through my head, one at a time. I was making conclusions and judgments as I phoned my oldest son Logan to let him know what had happened. As you might suspect, he started the habit of overthinking but took swift action to leave his house and go check on my father who was at the site of the crime. He told me within moments, to not try to stop him and I remembered why I wrote this book. He took aligned action and reminded me that I was the source of him cowering down during events that have been tragic, although none has been as tragic as this one. My heart was broken.

I used the tactics and tools you have been given in this book to help myself move through the experience by mixing up what I allowed my mind to do. I know from experience that the Law of Attraction is complete, and it cannot be disproven, so I made sure I didn't get into conversations too long, because I recognized the trigger element of this type of reaction. I was already involved pretty deeply, into overthinking about what may have really happened, you know? What was the motive, who was at fault? A million thoughts saturated my brain and mind.

I made sure that I referenced the fact I was indeed overthinking and did something more mindless. I downloaded an audio book called "The Biology of Belief" by Dr. Gregg Braden, one of my heroes, and listened intently to his words about how our Universe is created by a set of beliefs that the collective consciousness carries about the universe, and everything in it.

I made sure to alternate house cleaning, brain feeding, and overthinking so I could feel better and not get trapped in the feedback loop. I knew I would not be void of overthinking because a human-being lost their life, and because I was now dealing with the fact that it didn't hurt as bad as I thought it should. Trauma and numbness go hand-in-hand for me, so I have gotten pretty good at it. I did allow my emotions to come forth and I loved them through it.

ABOUT THE AUTHOR

Carla Wynn Hall, Self-Proclaimed Human Potential Activist, Inspired Creative Muse, mother, grandmother, and #1 International Bestselling Author!

From the northern tip of Alabama, Carla Wynn Hall was conceived and lived most of her life. She took her story of tragedy and turned it into a series of books for the generations, focusing on the unspoken quantum miracles that exist inside of the soul and the power of the human mind to manifest.

Her passion for diving deeply into the uncharted areas of the soul and mind, has led her to write books that continue to become bestsellers. Her drive to support those who have disabilities and have been tossed out by a society that judges and abandons – has allowed her to help over 2000 women become authors in her book programs.

"I know we are not put on earth to fight and kill one another in mindless wars, but that we are here to peacefully create new and delightful solutions for generations to come" – Carla Wynn Hall

MEDIA AND ORDERS

www.ingramcontent.com/pod-product-compliance
Lightning Source LLC
Chambersburg PA
CBHW071516220526
45472CB00003B/1041